i-SPY

dogs

SPY IT! SCORE IT!

Introduction

It is generally agreed nowadays that the many different breeds of dog are all descended from that great wild dog, the wolf. If you have ever watched the behaviour of wild wolves on wildlife films or even in zoos, you will realise that our cuddly household pets have many similar characteristics. Over the years, humans learned to breed dogs to carry out particular tasks. Some had strong herding instincts – and these became the shepherd dogs we know so well today.

Others were just good companions and became 'man's best friend'. Taking on a dog is a great responsibility. Dogs do not just need feeding – they require regular exercise (some need lots) to ensure their wellbeing. Many have coats that require a lot of care and most importantly, in order to be happy they need lots of loving attention. Remember that the character of the dog as described in this book should only be taken as a guide. Like all animals, including people, each dog is an individual with its own personality and temperament.

How to use your i-SPY book

Keep your eyes peeled for the i-SPYs in the book.

If you spy it, score it by ticking the circle or star.

Items with a star are difficult to spot so you'll have to search high and low to find them.

Once you score 1000 points, send away for your super i-SPY certificate. Follow the instructions on page 64 to find out how.

2

Brittany

Size Medium

Walks More than two hours a day

Grooming More than once a week

A busy dog, he is affectionate and has a pleasant nature. Easy to train, his dense, fine coat is not difficult to keep clean.

15 POINTS

English Setter

Size Large

Walks More than two hours a day

Grooming More than once a week

One of the most glamorous of all breeds, they make great working dogs as well as lovable companions.

TOP SPOT!

20 POINTS

German Pointer (SHORT-HAIRED)

Size Large

Walks More than two hours a day

Grooming Once a week

He is a highly trainable and shows real grace. He is a pleasure to watch, but you will get tired before he will!

 5 POINTS

German Pointer (WIRE-HAIRED)

Size Large

Walks More than two hours a day

Grooming More than once a week

Easily trained and friendly, he has a cheerful appearance, making him a good family dog and worker.

 **10** POINTS

Gordon Setter

Size Large

Walks More than two hours a day

Grooming More than once a week

He is trainable and an intelligent dog capable of enjoying all the exercise an owner can give him.

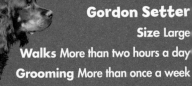

 10 POINTS

Hungarian Vizsla

Size Large

Walks More than two hours a day

 5 POINTS

Grooming Once a week

Being an intelligent, friendly dog, with a good memory, he is easy to train. He is a very popular pet in his native Hungary and can adapt to homes of all sizes.

 Vizslas are a very old breed, with the first written reference about them appearing in the 14th century.

Hungarian Vizsla (WIRE-HAIRED)

 **10 POINTS**

Size Large

Walks More than two hours a day

Grooming More than once a week

With a harsh wiry coat and bushy eyebrows, he can sometimes look a little bit stern but has the same friendly character as his smooth-coated cousin.

 For simplicity of reference it is common to use the male reference when referring to dogs.

Irish Red and White Setter

Size Large

Walks More than two hours a day

Grooming More than once a week

He is a good-natured dog who is happy to join in family activities – and he really enjoys his food! He has lots of energy, and once fully grown, he needs lots of space to run around.

TOP SPOT!

Irish Setter

Size Large

Walks More than two hours a day

Grooming More than once a week

His happy-go-lucky attitude is very endearing and his affectionate nature makes him a good household dog ready for all the fun a family will provide.

 10 POINTS

 10 POINTS

Italian Spinone

Size Large

Walks More than two hours a day

Grooming More than once a week

An easy dog to train, he will fit into the family environment. His thick and wiry coat is simple to keep in good condition and its texture means that he does not bring too much dirt inside.

Pointer

Size Medium

Walks More than two hours a day

Grooming Once a week

He has an even temper and is capable of fitting into a family but he is most at home out hunting on the moors.

> ℹ️ Pointers get their names from the fact that they alert their handler to hiding birds by pointing to them with their nose.

10 POINTS

Retriever (CHESAPEAKE BAY)

15 POINTS

Size Large

Walks More than two hours a day

Grooming Once a week

Endless energy, muscle power, a love of food and affection with a touch of independence, all go to produce a dog for the energetic family.

Retriever (CURLY-COATED)

TOP SPOT!

Size Large

Walks More than two hours a day

Grooming More than once a week

25 POINTS

His waterproof coat is well designed for his love of the outdoors; even after a swim, all it takes is a few quick shakes and he is practically dry.

Retriever (FLAT-COATED)

5 POINTS

Size Large

Walks More than two hours a day

Grooming More than once a week

He is a slow-maturing dog, who keeps his puppy-like qualities for several years. He is outgoing and eager to please.

Retriever (GOLDEN)

 5 POINTS

Size Large

Walks More than two hours a day

Grooming More than once a week

Goldens are easy to train, rarely fussy eaters and have a thick coat that is reasonably easy to keep clean. It is no surprise that the breed has become one of the most popular dogs.

 In 2006 there was a gathering of Golden Retrievers in Scotland (their original home) where a record-breaking photograph was taken of 188 Goldens in one image.

Retriever (LABRADOR)

Size Large

Walks More than two hours a day

Grooming Once a week

Labradors adore children and have a kind and loving nature and a confident air. City living is not really their scene – they are more at home in the countryside.

 Labradors have webbed toes, a thick otter-like tail and dense coats, making them fantastic swimmers in even the coldest of water.

 5 POINTS

Gundog

Retriever (NOVA SCOTIA DUCK TOLLING)

Size Medium

Walks Up to one hour a day

Grooming More than once a week

A handsome dog who makes an enthusiastic family companion for the active household. He enjoys dog sports such as agility and frisbee, and is easy to groom.

 10 POINTS

Spaniel (AMERICAN COCKER)

Size Medium

Walks More than two hours a day

Grooming Every day

He has a cheerful nature and makes a highly successful family dog, but needs careful grooming.

10 POINTS

Spaniel (CLUMBER)

Size Large

Walks Up to one hour a day

Grooming More than once a week

A well-mannered companion, he truly deserves greater popularity as he fits in well to family life.

TOP SPOT!

20 POINTS

The name 'cocker' is derived from the fact that these dogs were originally bred to disturb Woodcock for shooting.

5 POINTS Spaniel (COCKER)

Size Medium

Walks Up to one hour a day

Grooming Every day

A busy little dog who likes lots of exercise, thrives on human companionship and can often be found with a toy in his mouth, tail wagging furiously.

Spaniel (ENGLISH SPRINGER)

Size Medium

Walks More than two hours a day

Grooming More than once a week

Like so many of the gundog breeds, his cheerful outgoing nature makes him endearing and a popular choice as an energetic family companion.

In 1982, Bob, an English Springer Spaniel, stood for Parliament representing 'The Monster Raving Loony Barking Mad Dog Party'.

5 POINTS

11

Spaniel (FIELD)

25 POINTS

Size Medium

Walks More than two hours a day

Grooming More than once a week

This breed is most definitely not suited to city living – but he makes an excellent companion for people who prefer rural life.

TOP SPOT!

Spaniel (IRISH WATER)

Size Large

Walks More than two hours a day

Grooming More than once a week

He is by nature a very affectionate dog and has a distinct sense of humour. He makes a lovable family dog and never says no to a walk!

25 POINTS

TOP SPOT!

Spaniel (SUSSEX)

Size Medium

Walks More than two hours a day

Grooming More than once a week

His wrinkled brows can give him a frowning look but that is as far as the frown goes; he is capable of being an excellent family dog in a country household.

TOP SPOT!

25 POINTS

Spaniel (WELSH SPRINGER)

Size Medium

Walks More than two hours a day

Grooming More than once a week

The Welsh is somewhat smaller than the English Springer. He is also easier to keep clean – and his temperament is just as kind.

10 POINTS

Weimaraner

Size Large

Walks More than two hours a day

Grooming Once a week

With a silvery-grey coat and light-coloured eyes, the Weimaraner has increased in popularity.

5 POINTS

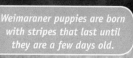

i *Weimaraner puppies are born with stripes that last until they are a few days old.*

13

Afghan Hound

Size Large

Walks More than two hours a day

Grooming Every day

Afghans have a tendency to be shy with strangers, but they are very affectionate and are faithful to their owner.

15 POINTS

TOP SPOT!

Basenji

20 POINTS

Size Small

Walks Up to one hour a day

Grooming Once a week

He is curious, self-confident and friendly, and becomes very attached to his human family. He loves to play but also likes to chew!

 Basenjis are known as the 'barkless dog' and show happiness with a crowing-yodelling noise.

Basset Griffon Vendeen (GRAND)

Size Medium

Walks More than two hours a day

Grooming Every day

This is a dog with a sense of humour who loves to join in human activity. Being a true hound, he has a tendency to be hard of hearing and is notorious for escaping!

15 POINTS

15 POINTS

Basset Griffon Vendeen (PETIT)

Size Medium

Walks Up to one hour a day

Grooming More than once a week

A typical hound, his happy, extrovert temperament helps make him a breed for the healthy, fun-loving family.

Basset Hound

Size Large

Walks Up to one hour a day

Grooming Once a week

The Basset deserves his popularity as a family dog; he is as happy curled up by the fire as he is romping in the garden.

10 POINTS

Hound

Beagle

Size Medium

Walks More than two hours a day

Grooming Once a week

He makes a first-class family pet –
a bustling, eager little dog, full of
enthusiasm and energy, ever ready
for any activity that involves him.

 The Peanuts character 'Snoopy' is often
described as the world's most famous Beagle.

Bloodhound

Size Large

Walks More than two hours a day

Grooming Once a week

He is generally good-natured and
affectionate but can be a
bit sensitive. He has a deep
loud voice that cannot be ignored.

 His amazing ability to follow a human scent over all types of terrain
for many hours has given the Bloodhound an almost super-canine
reputation, which has been promoted by writers of detective fiction.

Borzoi

15 POINTS

Size Large

Walks Up to one hour a day

Grooming More than once a week

The elegant, gentle Borzoi is laid-back and happy to relax with familiar people but can be sensitive to their surroundings and wary of strangers.

Dachshund (LONG-HAIRED)

15 POINTS

Size Medium

Walks Up to one hour a day

Grooming More than once a week

Dachshunds are active dogs and once fully mature, love lots of exercise!

Dachshund (MINIATURE LONG-HAIRED)

10 POINTS

Size Small

Walks Up to 30 minutes a day

Grooming More than once a week

Dachshunds are very happy snoozing on your lap. They are loyal companions and can make good family pets.

Dachshund (MINIATURE SMOOTH-HAIRED)

5 POINTS

Size Small

Walks Up to 30 minutes a day

Grooming Once a week

Dachshunds are not noted for their obedience but with patience and persistence they can be trained very well.

Dachshund (MINIATURE WIRE-HAIRED)

Size Small

Walks Up to 30 minutes a day

Grooming More than once a week

Dachshunds are most definitely small hounds and when they catch a scent they can 'go deaf' if it suits them!

10 POINTS

10 POINTS

Dachshund (SMOOTH-HAIRED)

Size Medium

Walks Up to one hour a day

Grooming Once a week

Their bark can be deep and people are often surprised to hear such a deep noise coming from a dog the size of a Dachshund.

Dachshund (WIRE-HAIRED)

10 POINTS

Size Medium

Walks Up to one hour a day

Grooming More than once a week

Dachshunds are scrappy little dogs that will gladly choose the role of a security guard and will send any unwelcome guests packing!

> *The name 'Dachshund' roughly translates as 'badger dog', as they were once used for hunting badgers. The smaller miniature varieties were used for hunting foxes and rabbits.*

Deerhound

Size Giant

Walks More than two hours a day

Grooming More than once a week

Dignity, humour, affection and loyalty all play their part in the temperament of this sensitive soul. But his true passion is for exercise – and plenty of it!

TOP SPOT!

20 POINTS

Foxhound

Size Large

Walks More than two hours a day

Grooming Once a week

As they were bred to live in packs, Foxhounds are happiest in the company of other dogs. They have to investigate everything – often with little thought for any furniture that may be in the way!

20 POINTS

TOP SPOT!

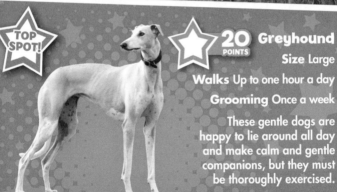

TOP SPOT!

20 POINTS

Greyhound

Size Large

Walks Up to one hour a day

Grooming Once a week

These gentle dogs are happy to lie around all day and make calm and gentle companions, but they must be thoroughly exercised.

 Despite there being thousands of racing Greyhounds, this breed is becoming very rare as there are few Greyhound breeders breeding for dog shows or domestic homes.

Irish Wolfhound

Size Giant

Walks More than two hours a day

Grooming More than once a week

In spite of his size, he is one of the gentlest of dogs with a proud yet calm expression.

10 POINTS

Otterhound

Size Large

Walks More than two hours a day

Grooming More than once a week

He is a kind fellow with a typical loud baying call. A dog for the energetic but not for the house-proud!

TOP SPOT!

25 POINTS

5 POINTS

Rhodesian Ridgeback

Size Large

Walks More than two hours a day

Grooming Once a week

He is an excellent family dog, good with children, affectionate and very loyal and protective of his family.

Hound

Saluki

Size Large

Walks More than two hours a day

Grooming Once a week

He is highly strung, very sensitive, very intelligent and extremely affectionate to those he loves. He is a great running companion.

15 POINTS

Whippet

Size Medium

Walks Up to one hour a day

Grooming Once a week

'Gentle' and 'affectionate' are an understatement – he loves the company of people.

5 POINTS

 It is thought that the name 'Whippet' comes from their quick movement and sharp nature – being like a 'little whip'.

Australian Cattle Dog

15 POINTS

Size Medium

Walks Up to one hour a day

Grooming Once a week

This dog has great stamina and although wary of strangers, he is protective of his family and makes a dutiful companion.

Australian Shepherd

Size Medium

Walks More than two hours a day

15 POINTS

Grooming More than once a week

He is intelligent and energetic but his territorial nature means he needs training and exercise.

10 POINTS ### Bearded Collie

Size Large

Walks Up to one hour a day

Grooming Every day

He is an active dog with a happy, outgoing nature – always ready for the next adventure!

23

Belgian Shepherd Dog (GROENENDAEL)

Size Medium

Walks More than two hours a day

Grooming More than once a week

15 POINTS

Belgian Shepherds are an active and intelligent breed. They are playful and love to chase but they need plenty of exercise.

Belgian Shepherd Dog (LAEKENOIS)

Size Medium

Walks More than two hours a day

Grooming More than once a week

Belgian Shepherds are not well suited to city-living; they are happiest in a rural setting and with 'work' to do – be that herding or learning new tricks!

20 POINTS

TOP SPOT!

Belgian Shepherd Dog (MALINOIS)

Size Medium

Walks More than two hours a day

Grooming More than once a week

15 POINTS

Belgian Shepherds are loyal and affectionate to their owners but can be wary of new people.

24

Belgian Shepherd Dog (TERVUEREN)

Size Medium

Walks More than two hours a day

Grooming More than once a week

20 POINTS

Owing to their intelligence, Belgian Shepherds need a lot of physical and mental stimulation. They were originally bred for herding, so don't be surprised to see them trying to herd cyclists or joggers when out for a walk!

TOP SPOT!

Border Collie

Size Medium

Walks More than two hours a day

Grooming More than once a week

He needs a lot of exercise, thrives on company and will always join in games. Dedicated to his family, he needs to work to be happy.

 5 POINTS

Briard

 15 POINTS

Size Large

Walks More than two hours a day

Grooming Every day

He is an extrovert who loves games and makes a good family dog.

 5 POINTS

Collie (ROUGH)

Size Large

Walks Up to one hour a day

Grooming Every day

This breed is more than just a pretty face – they were bred to work, and their strong herding instinct is still apparent today.

25 POINTS

Collie (SMOOTH)

Size Large

Walks Up to one hour a day

Grooming Once a week

This breed can be sensitive and reserved but he is gentle, affectionate and responsive to his owners.

TOP SPOT!

Finnish Lapphund

Size Medium

Walks Up to one hour a day

Grooming Every day

This breed is easy-going and loves to please his owners. He is gentle and enjoys the company of children.

15 POINTS

German Shepherd Dog

Size Large

Walks More than two hours a day

Grooming More than once a week

He is a very intelligent breed and needs to be kept busy – if not he is likely to become bored and mischievous!

5 POINTS

Lancashire Heeler

Size Small

Walks Up to one hour a day

Grooming Once a week

The Heeler is intelligent and eager to please, with a love of people; he enjoys being with children and especially likes joining in games.

TOP SPOT!

 20 POINTS

Old English Sheepdog

Size Large

Walks More than two hours a day

Grooming Every day

Intelligent and friendly, he is protective of his family and friends and has a particularly loud bark, which is likely to warn off any intruders!

10 POINTS

The most famous Old English is the iconic Dulux dog. All the dogs (except one) used in the adverts have been champions at Crufts!

Pyrenean Mountain Dog

Size Giant

Walks More than two hours a day

Grooming More than once a week

Once used as a guard dog, he has a very gentle side to his nature and is affectionate and tolerant with children, making him a popular house pet.

15 POINTS

Samoyed

Size Medium

Walks More than two hours a day

Grooming Every day

A true Sam is a friendly, positive, happy breed, which explains why he has earned the nickname 'smiley dog'.

10 POINTS

Shetland Sheepdog

Size Small

5 POINTS

Walks Up to one hour a day

Grooming Every day

This cheerful little dog always has to be 'on-the-go'. He is affectionate with his owner but a little reserved with strangers.

Pastoral

Welsh Corgi (CARDIGAN)

Size Medium

Walks Up to one hour a day

Grooming More than once a week

He gives the impression of being a restful character but is perfectly capable of becoming lively whenever he is asked to!

TOP SPOT!

 20 POINTS

Welsh Corgi (PEMBROKE)

Size Medium

Walks Up to one hour a day

Grooming More than once a week

He has a bark that is much bigger than his small size would suggest and can be prone to eating much more than is good for him!

 10 POINTS

Airedale Terrier

Size Large

Walks Up to one hour a day

Grooming Every day

An excellent family dog, particularly good with children and always ready to join in their games.

10 POINTS

Bedlington Terrier

10 POINTS

Size Medium

Walks Up to one hour a day

Grooming More than once a week

Despite appearances, he is a tough little dog, good in the house and makes a delightful family pet.

5 POINTS ### Border Terrier

Size Small

Walks Up to one hour a day

Grooming More than once a week

An active member of a family who has a temperament that combines good nature with a plucky spirit.

Terrier

Bull Terrier

Size Medium

Walks Up to one hour a day

Grooming Once a week

For all his standoffish appearance, he is in fact a very friendly dog who loves human company, even if he is prone to taking issue with the dog next door!

5 POINTS

 Bill Sykes's dog 'Bullseye' in the Charles Dickens novel 'Oliver Twist' was supposedly a Bull Terrier.

Bull Terrier (MINIATURE)

Size Medium

Walks Up to one hour a day

Grooming Once a week

They love their family and are playful, determined and feisty!

 20 POINTS

 TOP SPOT!

Cairn Terrier

Size Small

Walks Up to one hour a day

Grooming Once a week

5 POINTS

He loves people, is an able swimmer and a great hunter. Ready for any activity, he makes an ideal companion for a family.

Dandie Dinmont Terrier

20 POINTS

TOP SPOT!

Size Medium

Walks Up to one hour a day

Grooming More than once a week

An intelligent chap with a will of his own – not the most obedient of pets! Devoted to children, he can melt the hardest of hearts.

TOP SPOT!

Fox Terrier (SMOOTH)

Size Medium

Walks Up to one hour a day

Grooming Once a week

He is not the dog to let loose on a hillside covered with sheep but is ideally suited to family life in town.

20 POINTS

10 POINTS

Fox Terrier (WIRE)

Size Medium

Walks Up to one hour a day

Grooming More than once a week

He is alert, active, bold and is certainly not afraid to speak up for himself! Cheerful and happy, he makes an excellent family pet.

Glen of Imaal Terrier

Size Medium

Walks Up to one hour a day

Grooming More than once a week

He appears rough, but he is a gentle family companion, not nearly as noisy as many small terriers!

25 POINTS

TOP SPOT!

20 POINTS

Irish Terrier

Size Medium

Walks Up to one hour a day

Grooming More than once a week

A daredevil at heart, the Irish Terrier nevertheless has the softest, most gentle and loving character.

TOP SPOT!

Kerry Blue Terrier

Size Medium

Walks Up to one hour a day

Grooming Every day

An extrovert at heart, the Kerry is a spirited dog, determined but adaptable. He makes a good house pet, but also an excellent guard.

20 POINTS

Lakeland Terrier

Size Medium

Walks Up to one hour a day

Grooming More than once a week

A cheerful little rascal, he is hardy and agile as well as courageous, affectionate, tireless, lovable and naughty!

20 POINTS

Terrier

Manchester Terrier

Size Small

Walks Up to one hour a day

Grooming Once a week

He makes a great companion, very agile and not aggressive. He is devoted to his family and fits into any environment.

TOP SPOT!

20 POINTS

Norfolk Terrier

Size Small

Walks Up to one hour a day

Grooming More than once a week

He has a delightful personality and although totally fearless, is not one to normally start a fight.

10 POINTS

TOP SPOT!

20 POINTS

Norwich Terrier

Size Small

Walks Up to one hour a day

Grooming More than once a week

This breed are feisty little hunters, good watchdogs, responsive and loyal to their owners and usually friendly with strangers and other dogs.

Parson Russell Terrier

Size Medium

Walks Up to one hour a day

Grooming Once a week

He is best suited to country life and is too intelligent to be left on his own for long periods; he will get bored and could easily become destructive and noisy!

10 POINTS

Scottish Terrier

Size Medium

Walks Up to one hour a day

Grooming Once a week

His public image is often that of a serious 'Scottie' but to his family and friends he is affectionate and cheerful.

10 POINTS

Terrier

TOP SPOT!

Sealyham Terrier

Size Medium

Walks Up to one hour a day

Grooming Every day

Fit, active and ready to frolic and play, he makes an intelligent and charming companion.

25 POINTS

Soft-coated Wheaten Terrier

Size Medium

Walks Up to one hour a day

Grooming Every day

10 POINTS

Extrovert and energetic, this happy-go-lucky breed thrives on human companionship. He requires a little patience to train, but is eager to please.

Staffordshire Bull Terrier

Size Small

Walks Up to one hour a day

Grooming Once a week

Renowned for his courage, although to his family he is kind and his love of children is well known.

5 POINTS

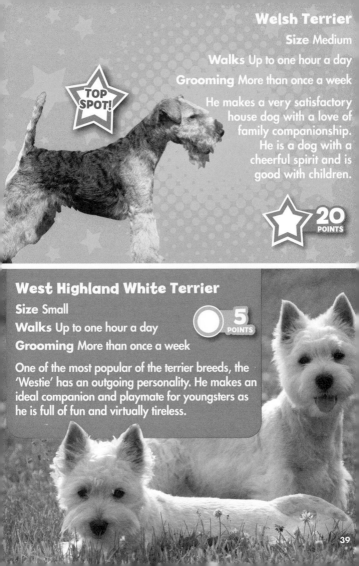

Welsh Terrier

Size Medium

Walks Up to one hour a day

Grooming More than once a week

He makes a very satisfactory house dog with a love of family companionship. He is a dog with a cheerful spirit and is good with children.

TOP SPOT!

20 POINTS

West Highland White Terrier

Size Small

Walks Up to one hour a day

Grooming More than once a week

5 POINTS

One of the most popular of the terrier breeds, the 'Westie' has an outgoing personality. He makes an ideal companion and playmate for youngsters as he is full of fun and virtually tireless.

Affenpinscher

15 POINTS

Size Small

Walks Up to one hour a day

Grooming More than once a week

Full of mischief, he is a lively little character, and his antics make him an entertaining companion.

Bichon Frise

5 POINTS

Size Small

Walks Up to one hour a day

Grooming Every day

A happy little dog who thrives on being the centre of attention. He is a complete extrovert.

Bolognese

15 POINTS

Size Small

Walks Up to one hour a day

Grooming Every day

He delights in family activities and expects to be included in long walks and games.

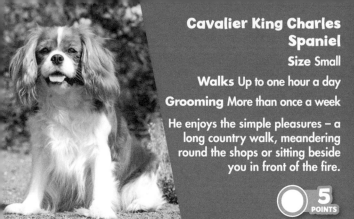

Cavalier King Charles Spaniel

Size Small

Walks Up to one hour a day

Grooming More than once a week

He enjoys the simple pleasures – a long country walk, meandering round the shops or sitting beside you in front of the fire.

5 POINTS

Chihuahua (LONG COAT)

Size Small

Walks Up to one hour a day

Grooming More than once a week

5 POINTS

He is a big dog at heart, but his small size makes him easy to take anywhere. He is highly intelligent and easily trained.

Chihuahua (SMOOTH COAT)

5 POINTS

Size Small

Walks Up to one hour a day

Grooming Once a week

Elderly people find him an ideal pet, happy to be a much-loved lap dog and also a good house dog, but he is not a suitable pet for small children.

Chinese Crested

10 POINTS

Size Small

Walks Up to one hour a day

Grooming Once a week

Affectionate and intelligent, they make unique and delightful companions and are good watchdogs.

English Toy Terrier (BLACK & TAN)

TOP SPOT!

25 POINTS

Size Small

Walks Up to one hour a day

Grooming Once a week

He makes a charming and intelligent companion, whose smooth, glossy coat requires minimal care.

Griffon Bruxellois

Size Small

Walks Up to one hour a day

Grooming More than once a week

This monkey-faced little dog is a constant source of amusement and delight to those who own him. His terrier-like qualities mean that he is happy to indulge in plenty of exercise.

15 POINTS

Italian Greyhound

Size Small

Walks Up to one hour a day

Grooming Once a week

Cheerful, brave and courageous, he has a gentle and loving nature. He is comfort-loving and will happily wrap himself in a blanket.

10 POINTS

10 POINTS

Japanese Chin

Size Small

Walks Up to one hour a day

Grooming More than once a week

Although he is a dainty little dog, he is in no way delicate. He is bright and intelligent, very stylish and extrovert and has a constant look of astonishment!

43

King Charles Spaniel

Size Small

Walks Up to one hour a day

Grooming More than once a week

20 POINTS

A true aristocrat, he is elegant and cheerful, and makes a very affectionate, devoted companion, while his large, dark eyes give him a soft, appealing expression.

TOP SPOT!

Lowchen (LITTLE LION DOG)

Size Small

Walks Up to one hour a day

Grooming More than once a week

15 POINTS

Affectionate, active and playful, he adapts well to city life and has many qualities that make him a popular family pet.

Maltese

10 POINTS

Size Small

Walks Up to one hour a day

Grooming Every day

He is merry, friendly and very intelligent. Hidden behind his glamorous appearance is a lively dog who is full of fun.

Miniature Pinscher

Size Small

Walks Up to one hour a day

Grooming Once a week

He is a lively and high-spirited dog with quick reactions and a great sense of hearing, which makes him a good little guard dog.

10 POINTS

Papillon

10 POINTS

Size Small
Walks Up to one hour a day
Grooming More than once a week

He is a lively breed requiring a lot of human company. He is happy, easy to teach and train and loves activities like agility.

Pekingese

10 POINTS

Size Small
Walks Up to one hour a day
Grooming Every day

Mischievous and playful, loving and sensitive, he is said to have the heart of a lion and shows this by guarding his toys and possessions.

Pomeranian

Size Small
Walks Up to one hour a day
Grooming More than once a week

Always eager to play, he is lighthearted, active, and sweet-tempered.

10 POINTS

Pug

Size Small

Walks Up to one hour a day

Grooming Once a week

A dignified dog, very intelligent, loves his family and is good-natured and sociable. He is robust and self-reliant, with great character and personality.

5 POINTS

Yorkshire Terrier

Size Small

Walks Up to one hour a day

Grooming Every day

His terrier-like qualities include a hunting instinct, be it for a toy in the house or a rodent in the garden. He loves games, and appreciates a good walk.

5 POINTS

 This breed comes from Yorkshire and Lancashire but is thought to have descended from a mix of breeds brought down from Scotland during the Industrial Revolution.

Akita

Size Large

Walks More than two hours a day

Grooming Once a week

Devoted and protective towards his owners, he is also very affectionate.

10 POINTS

Boston Terrier

5 POINTS

Size Small

Walks Up to one hour a day

Grooming Once a week

A smart looking breed, he is good tempered and a happy house dog – if a little boisterous!

5 POINTS

Bulldog

Size Small

Walks Up to one hour a day

Grooming Once a week

Although this delightfully 'ugly' dog is a little bit stubborn by nature, he is good-tempered and affectionate with children.

Chow Chow

Size Medium

Walks Up to one hour a day

Grooming Every day

The Chow is reserved, stand-offish and extremely loyal to his owner, with a tendency to be a one-person dog.

 Chow Chows have unusual dark blue tongues.

Dalmatian

Size Medium

Walks More than two hours a day

Grooming Once a week

An excellent companion and house dog, he is an active, agile dog, who enjoys plenty of exercise and is more suited to country life than the town.

5 POINTS

 Most Dalmatian puppies are born completely white and do not begin to develop their spots until they are around two weeks old.

Utility

French Bulldog

5 POINTS

Size Small

Walks Up to one hour a day

Grooming Once a week

A dog that enjoys his home comforts, he has a jolly and charming personality and is full of life, although he is not boisterous or noisy.

German Spitz (KLEIN)

15 POINTS

Size Small

Walks Up to one hour a day

Grooming Every day

An independent character with a happy outlook, he makes an ideal pet for old and young people.

German Spitz (MITTEL

15 POINTS

Size Smal

Walks Up to one hour a day

Grooming Every day

He is not a difficult breec to look after but his thick coat must be groomec thoroughly to keep him tidy

Japanese Shiba Inu

Size Small

Walks Up to one hour a day

Grooming Once a week

The Shiba Inu is one of the few ancient dog breeds that still exists and he was originally bred as a hunting dog. He's a very alert, small dog, that gives the impression of being interested in everything going on around him.

20 POINTS

TOP SPOT!

Utility

Japanese Spitz

15 POINTS

Size Medium

Walks Up to one hour a day

Grooming Every day

A small, nimble dog that doesn't need lots of food or exercise. His affectionate nature makes him an attractive household pet.

Keeshond

Size Medium

Walks Up to one hour a day

Grooming Every day

A hardy dog, he will let visitors know that their arrival has been detected but will then greet them as long-lost friends!

15 POINTS

Lhasa Apso

Size Small

Walks Up to one hour a day

Grooming Every day

He is independent and can be quite stubborn and wary of strangers but is very loving and affectionate to friends and family.

5 POINTS

Miniature Schnauzer

Size Small
Walks Up to one hour a day
Grooming More than once a week

His size makes him a popular town dog. Robust, hardy and agile, he is also very alert, warning of the approach of strangers to his property.

5 POINTS

Poodle (MINIATURE)

Size Small
Walks Up to one hour a day
Grooming Every day

A clown by nature and a born entertainer devoted to his family. He is capable of learning quickly and enjoys showing off.

10 POINTS

Poodle (STANDARD)

Size Large
Walks Up to one hour a day
Grooming Every day

He is loving and loyal and will always show his appreciation when he has been given a good grooming.

10 POINTS

53

Poodle (TOY)

Size Small

Walks Up to one hour a day

5 POINTS

Grooming Every day

Light-hearted, elegant, friendly and high-spirited, with a happy nature and home-loving instincts, he makes the ideal companion.

Schnauzer

15 POINTS

Size Medium

Walks Up to one hour a day

Grooming More than once a week

Gentle, patient and trustworthy with children, he is the ideal companion for an active person who is able to give him plenty of exercise.

5 POINTS

Shar-pei

Size Medium

Walks Up to one hour a day

Grooming Once a week

Despite his frowning expression, the Shar-Pei is a very affectionate dog, particularly towards people.

Boxer

Size Large

Walks More than two hours a day

Grooming Once a week

A gentle, quiet Boxer does not exist; he is extrovert and energetic, loyal and fun-loving and always happy to join family games!

5 POINTS

Bullmastiff

Size Large

Walks More than two hours a day

Grooming Once a week

Highly spirited, he makes a happy companion who is totally devoted to the members of his family.

5 POINTS

Dobermann

Size Large

Walks More than two hours a day

Grooming Once a week

A Dobermann has a very adaptable outlook to life and fits into a family well – and will readily take over the most comfortable chair in the house!

5 POINTS

57

Working

Dogue De Bordeaux

Size Large

Walks Up to one hour a day

Grooming Once a week

Despite his large size, he is surprisingly agile and able to jump considerable heights. He makes a loyal and affectionate member of the family.

 This breed was made famous by the film 'Turner and Hooch' where the big slobbery dog 'Hooch' was played by a Dogue de Bordeaux called Beasley.

 5 POINTS

Giant Schnauzer

Size Large

Walks More than two hours a day

Grooming Every day

He is slow to mature and can be rather bold, but he is trainable, a good house dog and a lovable pet.

 15 POINTS

Great Dane

Size Giant

Walks More than two hours a day

Grooming Once a week

His kind character, affection for children, devotion to his family and easy tolerance of other animals make him an excellent house dog.

5 POINTS

i 'Scooby Doo' is generally believed to be a Great Dane, and was drawn for Hanna-Barbera by animator Iwao Takamoto, who based his illustrations on sketches of the pet Dane of a colleague.

Leonberger

Size Giant

Walks More than two hours a day

Grooming More than once a week

A naturally powerful dog with an even temper, though not as massive as his peers.

10 POINTS

Working

15 POINTS

Mastiff

Size Giant

Walks Up to one hour a day

Grooming Once a week

A very intelligent dog, he is not excitable but is affectionate towards his owner and requires plenty of human contact

Newfoundland

Size Giant

Walks Up to one hour a day

Grooming Every day

This gentle giant is eager to please and makes a very suitable companion for children, joining in their games.

10 POINTS

Portuguese Water Dog

Size Medium

Walks Up to one hour a day

Grooming Every day

15 POINTS

He is a friendly dog, even if he can be self-willed. He needs firm handling when young to overcome this stubborn streak

Rottweiler

5 POINTS

Size Large

Walks More than two hours a day

Grooming Once a week

He is strong and imposing but easily obedience trained and enjoys working. He has natural guarding instincts, but is not aggressive by nature.

> *i* Many Rottweilers are very vocal and quite often 'talk' to their owners by moaning and grumbling, which may be mistaken for growling.

Russian Black Terrier

Size Large

Walks More than two hours a day

Grooming Every day

This is a dog that will stop trespassers in their tracks, but despite this he is not aggressive and has a friendly nature.

15 POINTS

Working

St. Bernard

5 POINTS

Size Giant

Walks Up to one hour a day

Grooming More than once a week

St. Bernards are very kind-hearted dogs – just as well, because the idea of an extremely large grumpy St. Bernard doesn't bear thinking about!

Siberian Husky

10 POINTS

Size Medium

Walks More than two hours a day

Grooming More than once a week

He has a delightful temperament and loves humans. His downfall is that he is a natural hunter – his prey may include the family cat or rabbit and he cannot be trusted off-lead!

15 POINTS

Tibetan Mastiff

Size Giant

Walks Up to one hour a day

Grooming More than once a week

Owing to his heritage as a guard dog of livestock, he can be distrustful of strangers – but he is generally friendly.

Index

i-SPY How to get your i-SPY certificate and badge

Let us know when you've become a super-spotter with 1000 points and we'll send you a special certificate and badge!

Here's what to do:

- Ask a grown-up to check your score.

- Apply for your certificate at
  www.collins.co.uk/i-SPY
  (if you are under the age of 13 we'll need
  a parent or guardian to do this).

- We'll email your certificate and
  post you a brilliant badge!